Daddy Promises

Kerry Arquette

Illustrated by Kevin McCain

CONCORDIA PUBLISHING HOUSE • SAINT LOUIS

Paperback Edition first printed 2005
Text copyright © 1999 Kerry Arquette
Illustrations copyright © 1999 Concordia Publishing House
Published by Concordia Publishing House
3558 S. Jefferson Avenue, St. Louis, MO 63118-3968

Image references for pages 24 and 25 is from The Stock Market/Bryan F. Peterson;
pages 20 and 21 is from Photo Disc; and page 32 is from Tony Stone Images/Joe Polillio

Manufactured in the United States of America

1 2 3 4 5 6 7 8 9 10   14 13 12 11 10 09 08 07 06 05

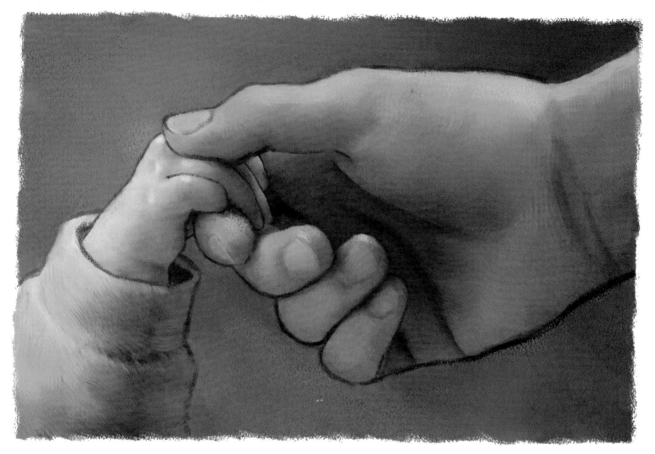

God sends another heartbeat into the world, another body, another soul.
A child is born!
It's a time for rejoicing.
It's a time for resolutions.
It's a time for making promises
that will take a lifetime to fulfill.

God has
placed
you in
my care.

I will be here
as you sleep…
and
I will be here
when
you wake.

I will
always be
here for
you,
whether
you can
see me
or not.

I promise.

I will listen with my heart and not just my ears.

Sometimes ears hide.

I will mend teddy bear holes and remind you that puppies like to chew. I will show you that kisses and bandages can fix most anything.

I will accept
the fact that we
may not always
see eye to eye.

From way up here
I can see far, but
from where you
stand, you can
see important little
things that my
up-in-the-air
eyes miss.

I will teach you right fr
only washable markers unt

rong and will buy
u learn the difference.

I will show you how to tie your shoes,
how to whistle,

and how to catch a high fly.

I will say I'm sorry
and ask you to forgive me
when I've hurt you.
Sometimes even good dads
make mistakes.

There is only one
perfect Father,
our Father in heaven.

I will read
wonderful, true
stories to you
about the world's
beginning,
a terrible flood and
a sturdy ark,
a Savior born
in a stable, and
a miraculous
resurrection.

I will teach you th

ks are more important than just words on a page.

I will be your biggest fan.

I will cheer just as loudly
when you're losing
as when you're winning.

I will teach you
that giving
is more important
than taking and
that God asks us
to help others.

I will explain that God filled the world with different kinds of people and different colors of people. He loves them all the same.

This makes the world a more interesting and beautiful place.

I will laugh at "knock-knock" jok
and "Why did the chicken
cross the road?" jokes,
if you will laugh with me.

I will not yell if you lea

our bike out in the rain.

I will let you
learn about
rust and
responsibility …
and that *walking*
to school takes
a long time!

I will learn
from you
things
that I've
forgotten …

that trees are for climbin

that everybody needs a secret hideout,

nd that pockets are for rocks.

I will be there
when your
good friend isn't
acting good at all.
I'll say, "The
world is full of
best friends you
haven't met yet."

I will teach you about Jes

ur very best Friend, who will never forsake you.

I will kiss and hug your bad dreams away ...

but I'll never kiss

in front of your friends.

I will teach you
how to talk to God,
and I will teach you
to listen
so you can hear
when God
talks to you.

I will tell
you the truth.

The truth is
that I love you.

God loves you.

I will tell you so
every day,
every *single* day.

I promise.